TELL ME ABOUT WRITERS AND ILLUSTRATORS

SHIRLEY HUGHES

written by
Chris Powling

Evans

Evans Brothers Limited

Published by Evans Brothers Limited
2A Portman Mansions
Chiltern Street
London W1M 1LE

Editor: Victoria Brooker
Design: Neil Sayer and Mark Holt
Production: Jenny Mulvanny
Photography: Richard Mewton except page 8 Alan Towse, page
9 (top left) Hulton Getty (bottom right) Corbis/Everett

Printed by Graficas Reunidas SA, Spain

British Library Cataloguing in Publication data.

Powling, Chris
  Tell me about Shirley Hughes
  1. Hughes, Shirley, 1929- – Biography – Juvenile literature
  2. Women novelists, English – 20th century – Biography – Juvenile
  literature 3. Novelists, English - 20th century -
  Biography - Juvenile literature
  I. Title II. Shirley Hughes
  823.9'14

ISBN 0237520397

Have you ever lost a favourite toy?

If so, I hope you've read a book called 'Dogger'. It was written and drawn by Shirley Hughes. "Dogger was a small, stuffed animal," says Shirley. "He'd belonged to one of my sons who couldn't bear to part with him."

'Dogger' became the story of a favourite toy which gets lost... then, thank goodness, is found again. All over the world children loved it. Ever since, Shirley has been famous.

This book tells you all about her.

Shirley's favourite place... at her drawing board.

Shirley Hughes was born in 1927. She grew up in the seaside town of West Kirby. This is near Liverpool where her father owned a big shop. He died when Shirley was only four.

'Easedale' - the house where Shirley grew up. She's the baby in the pram.

Shirley on her mother's lap, with her father and sisters.

Shirley's mother made sure she had a happy childhood. With her sisters, Brenda and Val, Shirley was always busy. "We played. We mucked about. We dressed up. We made up stories, as well, and acted them to anyone who would watch. We did a lot of writing, too, and a lot of drawing. Also a lot of reading."

Shirley, Brenda and Val. Shirley was the youngest and smallest of the three.

With the family at the seaside.

Shirley started school at Miss Todd's. "She was a scary lady but a wonderful teacher. Next, I went to West Kirby High School. I was good at English, History and Art. But not Maths or Science!"

Then the Second World War began. England was fighting Germany from 1939 to 1945.

West Kirby High School

Shirley on the tambourine at Miss Todd's.

Some children in wartime being taught how to put on a gas mask.

One of Shirley's favourite film stars was Buster Keaton.

Shirley remembers these years very clearly. "I went to school carrying a gas mask. I did air-raid drills. And I slept under the stairs at night because people said this was safer. Sometimes the war was frightening. Mostly, for me, it was dull."

It wasn't dull at the cinema, though. Or reading the comics brought here by American soldiers.

These were a good start for someone who loved stories. Especially stories that were told in pictures.

Students at the Ruskin School of Art in Oxford. The circle shows Shirley.

'The Witch That Wasn't'. A book written and drawn by Shirley as a student.

Shirley made up her mind to study Art. First, she went to college in Liverpool, then to the famous Ruskin School in Oxford. At Ruskin she spent hours and hours really learning how to draw. Already, deep down, she hoped to be an illustrator.

Shirley moved to London to get some work. Her first job was a pony story. She hated this because a pony had once bitten her. The publisher didn't use these drawings. Luckily they asked Shirley to draw some children for another story instead. This was her first book to be published.

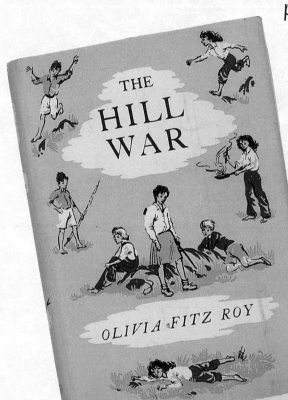

THE
HILL
WAR

OLIVIA FITZ ROY

The first of Shirley's book covers...

...and her 'roughs' for the same book.

Slowly, Shirley's book covers and black-and-white illustrations began to be noticed. She was especially pleased to work with Dorothy Edwards, author of the 'My Naughty Little Sister' series.

Already, she'd started writing her own stories - with pictures she'd drawn herself. The first of these was called 'Lucy and Tom's Day'. Children liked it so much, Shirley wrote more stories about Lucy and Tom.

Noel Streatfeild's books were famous. She asked Shirley to be her illustrator.

The first book drawn and written by Shirley.

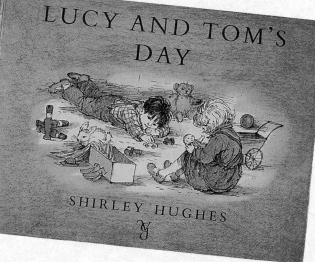

Shirley and John with their children Ed, Tom and Clara. Clara now writes and illustrates her own books.

All this was very hard work. "By now I was married," Shirley says. "I had three children of my own. It wasn't easy to keep on drawing with two boys and a girl at home."

Shirley's husband John was an architect. "Luckily, he loved drawing as much as I did. Often, at the weekend, he'd look after the family. This left me free to catch up with my work. Without John's help, I'd never have kept going."

But keep going she did.

Shirley's most famous book

Then, in 1977, came 'Dogger'. This wasn't just a world best-seller. It also won Shirley the Kate Greenaway Medal. This is the prize every illustrator wants to win.

After this came more books and more prizes. You can decide for yourself which book is the best. Is it 'Up and Up', or a 'Trotter Street' story, or one of Shirley's longer picture books, 'The Lion and the Unicorn'?

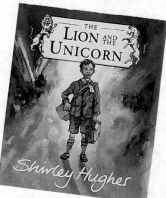

One of Shirley's books for older children

The children in her stories are not real, they come out of her imagination. But she gets a lot of her ideas for stories from the real children she knows.

'Alfie' is one of Shirley's best loved characters

Shirley reading with two of her grandchildren, Elsa and Alice. Her other grand-children are Paul, Adam, Jack, Martha and Claudia.

Sometimes, Shirley takes her work to the quiet of the Sussex countryside. Mostly, though, she works in London. She and John have lived in the same house for more than forty years.

Here, in an upstairs room, Shirley spends five or six hours each day.

Shirley in the London workroom where she has produced most of her books.

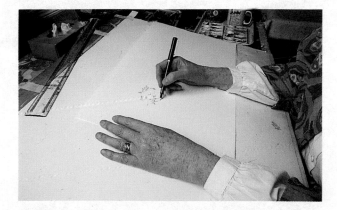

"While I'm writing the words," says Shirley, "my brain is already filling up with pictures. Then comes a 'rough'. I draw this very fast with felt pen or a pencil. I'm really excited as I do it."

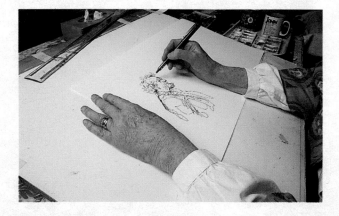

A quick sketch by Shirley - in this case drawing the writer of this book!

First come the roughs...

...then the finished picture

"The coloured picture takes much longer than the rough. Colour gives the story its mood. But I mustn't lose that excitement."

It's the same excitement she wants to pass on to her readers.

Of course, lots of other things also keep Shirley busy. She may be appearing at a Book Fair. Or on radio or television. Or helping with a book like this one. In 1999, the Queen gave her an honour called the OBE. This was a thank-you to Shirley for doing so much for children's reading.

A slice of cake to celebrate Shirley's OBE.

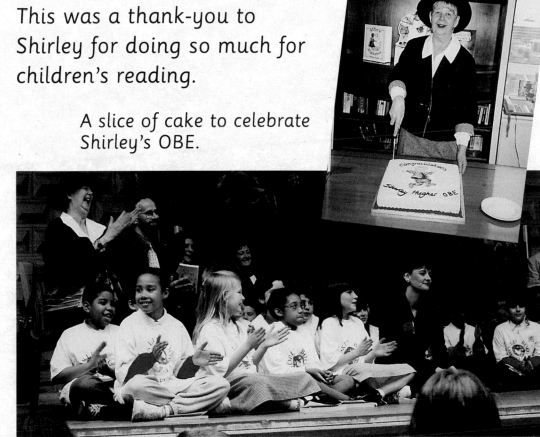

World Book Day 1998. Shirley is on stage with Cherie Blair, (sat bottom right) wife of the Prime Minister.

But Shirley stills likes illustrating best. Wherever she goes, she often takes a pencil and notebook. So does her husband John. "He'll be drawing the buildings," Shirley laughs. "And I'll be drawing the people."

So watch out for her.

After all, you never know. That girl or boy she's sketching could be you.

Shirley with her husband John, on a recent tour of American libraries.

Important dates

1927	Shirley Hughes was born
1932	She begins at Miss Todd's school
1938	Shirley goes to West Kirby School
1939-45	The Second World War
1944	Shirley studies at Liverpool Art School
1946	She transfers to The Ruskin School, Oxford
1950	She starts work as an illustrator
1952	Shirley marries John Vulliamy, an architect
1960	'Lucy and Tom's Day' is published
1976	'Helpers' wins the 'Other Award'
1977	'Dogger' wins the Kate Greenaway Medal
1980	Her work for children and books wins Shirley the Eleanor Farjeon Award
1980-99	Shirley's books become more and more popular world-wide - selling over 8 million copies
1999	Shirley is awarded the OBE

A drawing from one of Shirley's famous 'Alfie' books

Keywords

Architect
A person who draws and plans buildings

Kate Greenaway Medal
A top prize for children's book illustration

OBE
Order of the British Empire

Prime Minister
the person in charge of running the country

Publisher
someone who organises the printing of a book

Rough
The first draft of a picture book

Index